dramasc

CW00502599

Carrigan Street

by

JOHN PICK

Nelson

Thomas Nelson and Sons Ltd
Nelson House Mayfield Road
Walton-on-Thames Surrey
KT12 5PL UK

Nelson Blackie
Wester Cleddens Road
Bishopbriggs
Glasgow
G64 2NZ

Thomas Nelson (Hong Kong) Ltd
Toppan Building 10/F
22a Westlands Road
Quarry Bay Hong Kong

Thomas Nelson Australia
102 Dodds Street
South Melbourne
Victoria 3205 Australia

Nelson Canada
1120 Birchmount Road
Scarborough Ontario
M1K 5G4 Canada

FOREWORD

Drama is one of the most exciting of all forms of human activity. At its best, it involves us completely — whether we are acting ourselves or watching others act — and those occasions when we are gripped by some dramatic tension may be among the most memorable moments in our lives. In this new series we hope to encourage this sort of experience.

DRAMASCRIPTS are intended for use in secondary schools, amateur theatrical groups and youth clubs. The plays range widely from established classics to new works and adaptations of books and film scripts. There is nothing in any of the plays that is beyond the capabilities of younger actors. They may be used in a variety of ways: read privately for pleasure or aloud in groups, acted in the classroom, church hall or youth club, or in public performances. The maximum enjoyment is obviously to be found in actual performance — and the benefits of acting need no elaboration — but we have borne in mind that the play must interest and entertain however it is used, and we are confident that even the solitary reader will find here something of the excitement of the live theatre.

GUY WILLIAMS
Advisory Editor

CARRIGAN STREET

THE CHARACTERS

NEVIS, the old Night Watchman
SAMMY, a cheerful workman
GINGER, a miserable one
MORE, the quiet one
BLACKBIRD, the Union man
FOREMAN, the man in charge
OTHER WORKMEN

MR. ALLISS, of the Architect's Department
MR. ADAMSON, the Town Clerk
MISS STANLEY, his secretary
INSPECTOR HARGREAVES, head of the town force
W. P. C. SMITH
TWO BAILIFFS

THE EDITOR of the *Post*
CAROL, his secretary
PENNY, a new receptionist
T.V. INTERVIEWER
REPORTERS
CAMERAMEN
PHOTOGRAPHERS

THE WOMAN
MRS. MALONEY
MRS. FRANCIS
MRS. SPENCER
MRS. WRIGHT
MRS. PRICE
MRS. MARKS
HOUSEWIVES

The play is set on a motorway building site, and in
various offices in a large English town.

SCENE ONE

(Morning, **Sammy** *is hanging up his coat in the shed)*

Sammy. Time you were off! It's half past eight.

(He walks slowly round to where **Nevis** *sits)*

Sammy. Time for bed. It's morning.

Nevis. There's three of them red lamps gone in the night. I shall have to report it.

Sammy. Save your breath. Head Office isn't worried about a bit of pilfering. Just collect three more from the depot.

Nevis. No respect for what belongs to others, have you?

Sammy. Them lamps didn't belong to you, did they? They belong to the ratepayers, and one of the ratepayers borrowed three of them — that's all.

Nevis. They'll nick anything now. When the cement comes tomorrow they'll nick that. They'll nick shovels. They'll nick sand. One time we even lost a dozen of them red flags. Now who wants red flags, d'you reckon?

Sammy. Engine drivers. Let me help you on with your coat.

Nevis. You don't care about others' property, do you? It's all a joke to you — that's what I'm saying.

Sammy. That's right Ben old lad — just a joke.

Nevis. You won't take things seriously — that's where you go wrong.

1

Can't walk down a street now without getting your skull cracked open by some young thug after your wallet, and all your sort do is laugh.

Sammy. What can I do about it? I knock down houses and I build motorways. I work for the council. Honest Sam, that's me. I'm not in politics am I?

Nevis. Starting today are you?

Sammy. That's right. Last stretch of the inner ring road.

Nevis. Well just watch out — that's all.

Sammy. What do you mean by that Ben?

Nevis. Like I say, watch out. People are getting fed up with being thrown out of their homes just to make room for your precious motorways. It's just something I heard, that's all.

Sammy. Don't worry yourself old lad. When you come back tonight we'll have these houses flat on the ground. Just a heap of rubble.

(**Blackbird** *is hurrying towards them*)

Nevis. I'm off up to Head Office to report about them lamps. I know my duty even if you don't.

Sammy. You forgot your sandwich tin, Ben.

Ben. Oh — thanks.

Sammy. There you are. If I hadn't seen it lying there you'd have told the police it had been stolen, wouldn't you? I can see the headlines — 'Armed Thugs make off with sandwich tin in daring midnight raid'.

Nevis. You're so sharp you'll cut yourself.

Sammy. Mind how you go Ben.

2

(He hobbles off)

Blackbird. The bulldozer hasn't arrived. I've rung Head Office. They say it left the depot on time. But you can't trust them.

Sammy. I expect it's caught in a traffic jam. There was a big pile-up by the war memorial when I came through.

Blackbird. I don't think they've sent it. You can't trust the bosses. If it doesn't come we shall lose a day's work. And overtime.

Sammy. Plots — that's all you think about, isn't it? Why don't you trust people Blackbird — try to have a sunny, trusting character like I have.

*(***Ginger*** enters, in his usual foul mood)*

Ginger. Don't you lot talk to me. I've got a splitting headache. I've smoked twenty Park Drive and I can't shift it.

(The other workmen are drifting in, taking off coats, collecting shovels, stamping their feet to keep warm)

More. How did United do Ginger? I thought they were going to wipe the floor with City.

Ginger. Don't talk to me about United. It's not a new keeper they want — it's a new team. Sell this lot to Woolworths as shop assistants.

More. They wouldn't have the energy to open the till Ginger . . .

Ginger. Listen handsome. Don't talk like that.

*(He grabs ***More's*** lapel)*

Ginger. If anybody's going to make fun of United, I am. They're my team. I don't want you pushing your horrible little views in, see. You'll get your hooter flattened.

Foreman. Cut it out, you two. Save your energy for knocking them houses down.

Sammy. Carrigan Street . . .

Foreman. What do you say Sammy?

Sammy. Carrigan Street. Just about ten feet up that wall, above the boards where the kids have been chalking, you can make out the sign. It was called Carrigan Street. Must have been home to somebody once. And we're going to smash straight through 'em.

Blackbird. When the bulldozer arrives we are. Where is it?

Sammy. Bet they've sent it to the wrong site. They don't know what they're doing at Head Office. Remember that time at Nottingham when all we had to do was fit two taps, and they sent three cranes over from Derby?

Foreman. Glad you think it was funny.

More. It was a laugh though, that job. Somebody came and moved the diversion sign in the night and when we got there next morning half the traffic in Nottingham was on the bowling greens.

Sammy. That reminds me. Mr. Nevis reckons that somebody pinched three red lights in the night.

Foreman. They're up by the lorries. I saw them as I came in. He'll forget his own name next.

(Mrs. Maloney, and Mrs. Francis, both in headscarves, nervously approach Blackbird)

Mrs. Maloney. Excuse me — could you tell us who's in charge here?

Blackbird. Him over there.

Mrs. Maloney. Thank you. You're in charge of these men are you?

Foreman. I am missus. What can I do for you?

Mrs. Maloney. You've come to knock down Carrigan Street to build the inner ring road.

4

Foreman. That's right. As soon as the equipment comes, that is exactly what we're going to do.

Mrs. Francis. I think that you're wrong.

Foreman. What did you say?

Mrs. Francis. You're wrong. We think you're wrong.

Mrs. Maloney. We've come to tell you. We represent the Carrigan Street Society.

Foreman. Look Missus, as far as I'm concerned, you can represent Outer Mongolia. Just so long as you don't get in my way.

Mrs. Francis. You don't understand. We represent the Carrigan Street Society. We aim to stop the motorway being built. We don't want our houses knocked down.

Foreman. Now I don't want to get mixed up in politics. All I know is the council's told me to knock them houses down, and to build the motorway — and that is what I am going to do.

Mrs. Francis. You are not! We think this endless building of roads has to stop.

Mrs. Maloney. In fifty years time the motor car will be finished, but human beings won't. We say — leave people their houses and let the cars go elsewhere!

Sammy. It's no use complaining to us love — we are only the workmen.

Blackbird. You've been sent the proper forms, haven't you? There's been letters sent? Proper notification? It's all been done according to the book?

Mrs. Maloney. Of course it has.

Blackbird. Well then, it's all down in black and white. Don't trust anybody till it's down in black and white. Then don't trust 'em unless they stick to it. That's what I think.

Foreman. The council does stick to its agreements though. And anyway you can always complain at the office at the proper time.

Mrs. Francis. And what good does that do? They send out some well-dressed youth to talk to you. He gives you a cup of tea and sits and listens. But all the time you can tell he isn't really taking it in — his eyes are on the clock behind you. He's decided he'll give you half an hour.

Mrs. Maloney. At the end of half an hour he shows you out. Says he'll look into it. Then about a week after that they send you a letter and of course nothing's been changed. Only they've given you your chance to say your piece you see.

Foreman. Now look, you're a sensible pair. Be reasonable. Every second job we do we get this sort of carry-on. People hang banners over the street, threaten to kill themselves. You always feel a bit sorry but, in the end, you can't stand in the way of progress.

Mrs. Francis. You've been brainwashed. Building motorways everywhere isn't progress. It's how you live that matters, not how fast you travel.

Foreman. The authorities will win in the end.

Mrs. Maloney. I'm not so sure. There's plenty you can do to make their lives difficult.

Mrs. Francis. We can move back into the houses for a start. Your blokes didn't board 'em up too well. We can still live in them houses!

Foreman. Nothing wrong with the houses missus — but they're in the wrong place.

Mrs. Maloney. First house along — that belongs to Miss Ray. Lives on her own, bless her. Then there's my house. Then the Simpson twins — big lads they are. Oh, you're going to have plenty of trouble from us.

Ginger. You're a couple of lunatics if you want my view. Ought to be put inside, you did.

Mrs. Francis. We've invited the television to come. And the newspapers.

Mrs. Maloney. Just to see fair play. Not that we've anything against you lot personally.

Mrs. Francis. If you had any guts you'd join us. Remember — it could be your houses they take next.

(They go; the men look to the **Foreman** *for a lead)*

Ginger. Clowns they are. Lucky if they don't get a bashing.

Foreman. Well, it's nothing to do with us. It's an argument between them and the council. Let's get the shovels unloaded.

(**Alliss** *strides towards them, carrying a rolled-up plan)*

Sammy. Look out lads — Alliss is here. Look as if you're working.

Alliss. What's going on? You should have started by now.

Ginger. Haven't got the bulldozer, have we?

Blackbird. Head Office that is. We haven't been able to start work. Should have been here. In black and white, it was. Bulldozer to Inner Ring Site Five.

Foreman. And there's been a spot of trouble Mr. Alliss. The residents round here have been talking to us. They've formed a Society to stop the road being built. Say they're going to stop us knocking down Carrigan Street.

Alliss. They always say that. Take no notice.

Foreman. Well, they seem well-organised. I don't know whether they're bluffing, but they reckoned that the television boys and the newspaper people were coming down. It could look bad if there's any bother.

7

Alliss. What do they say they're going to do?

Foreman. I'm not quite sure. They seemed to say that there were still people living in them houses. Said there was a woman in the first. Old Miss Ray, I reckon they called her.

Ginger. Pull it down. On top of her? Best thing, d'you reckon?

Sammy. You ought to be in the army Ginger.

More. He ought to be in a zoo. With the other apes.

Alliss. I'd better see what Head Office thinks about this. Look, don't do anything. Just unload the shovels and sit tight. I'll get instructions.

Foreman. Can't do much without the bulldozer anyway.

(Sharp blast on the whistle)

Alliss. What is it Blackbird?

Blackbird. I must ask you whether my members will be getting the agreed rate during this period of enforced idleness.

Alliss. Of course they will. There's absolutely no question about it. We shall stick to the agreement.

Blackbird. That's all right then. As long as it's clear what's in black and white. All right lads. You can sit down. Union and Management have agreed.

Sammy. All right if I blow my nose is it Blackbird?

Alliss. If the television people do turn up, say nothing. I'll be back.

(He hurries away. The men settle down)

More. I wonder if there really are people behind those shutters. It seems very quiet.

Sammy. There won't be. There isn't any water, or gas. It's all been turned off. I think they were bluffing.

More. I've never heard such rubbish.

Sammy. I'm not so sure about it lad. In fifty years' time the motor car will be finished. We'll have to fly about in little helicopter things. And all these motorways will be cracked and covered with weeds. Just like canals are now.

Ginger. You'll be dead by then Sammy boy. Why bother?

Sammy. I suppose in a way she's right. People are more important than cars.

More. It's people that drive cars. It's ordinary people that *want* motorways.

Ginger. You're going soft in the head. You'll be writing articles for women's magazines next. Spare a thought for the old folk! You great nit!

Sammy. I just said I wasn't so sure about it. That's all. I was just thinking . . .

(They drink tea, chat, play cards and sit waiting . . .)

SCENE TWO

(In the business-like council offices the Town Clerk, **Adamson,** *is on the 'phone)*

Adamson. Your worship, I am really very sorry. It's disgraceful. I'll see to it at once, and please accept my apologies, and my assurance that it certainly won't happen again.

(He puts down the 'phone)

Adamson. Stupid old twit. Miss Stanley!

(His secretary enters)

Stanley. Yes Mr. Adamson?

Adamson. That, Miss Stanley, was the Mayor. His car was delayed this
morning in the one-way system for twenty minutes. Apparently
the traffic department has changed the one way system over the
weekend so that it kept bringing the cars out on to the by-pass and
the by-pass kept bringing them back on to the one-way system. He
went past his office three times, he says, but couldn't stop.

Stanley. I'm sorry to hear that Mr. Adamson.

Adamson. So am I. Let me have one of my pills – there, that's better!
The Mayor wants to know when the inner ring road will be
complete Miss Stanley. We shall have to write him a letter.

Stanley. We wrote one to him a fortnight ago on the same subject Mr.
Adamson. Shall I copy it out and send that again?

Adamson. Yes, do that.

(The telephone rings)

Stanley. Good morning, this is the Town Clerk's office. Mr. Adamson's
secretary speaking. Yes? Yes? Yes? No!

(She puts the receiver down)

Stanley. It was from a lady Mr. Adamson. She said she was representing
the Carrigan Street Society.

Adamson. She can't be. We're pulling Carrigan Street down.

Stanley. Well, you'd better be prepared for a shock. She rang up to say
that this society has – has hi-jacked one of our bulldozers.

Adamson. It has done – what?

Stanley. Apparently you sent a bulldozer this morning from the depot to the new inner ring site. It left at eight o'clock, but it didn't arrive. The caller said that we'd never find it . . .

Adamson. Get the Police — get on to Inspector Hargreaves! This is England, not the Wild West.

Stanley. She said something else. She said, tell Adamson that if he doesn't take his greasy hands off Carrigan Street there's worse to come!

SCENE THREE

(At the reception desk of the Post, **Alliss** *is arguing with a new receptionist)*

Alliss. All right — I know that you aren't supposed to disturb the Editor unless it's a matter of life and death, but this *is* a matter of life and death.

Penny. How do I know? My orders are that he's not to be disturbed. He's got somebody important with him.

Alliss. This is urgent. It's an urgent story for the *Post.* If you don't let me in to him you'll get into trouble. Can't you understand, you stupid girl, that this is an emergency?

Penny. Don't you start telling me what to do! How do I know who you are anyway. For all I know you've come to blow the building up. I have my orders, and I'm going to see they're carried out.

Alliss. Look — there are troublemakers in the town. It's important I give your Editor the facts before the — the other side get at him. Can't you please — please — use all your charm and intelligence and just arrange for me to see him for two minutes? I know him quite well. I assure you he'll be pleased to see me.

11

Penny. Will the Sports Editor do? He's not doing anything. He's written his report on the big match last night.

Alliss. It's nothing to do with sport. I couldn't care less about the big match.

Penny. I went. Oooh it was good. City scored from a penalty a minute from the end. I was so excited I bit my handbag strap in two.

Alliss. Can I speak to him on the 'phone then?

Penny. Well you can't just now. He's got the Carrigan Street Society people with him just now. Have you heard about that? The Council is going to tear their houses down on top of them. I think it's awful. I'd like to scratch their eyes out.

Alliss. It is vital that I see him. Ring him up. Make an appointment. I must see him as soon as he finishes with these people — heaven knows what nonsense they're telling him.

Penny. I think they're rather nice. My Aunt Bridget lives down that way — I'm all for them. In fact I have heard a rumour — I don't know whether I ought to tell you — a rumour that they've got a bomb wired to each house. Soon as the bulldozers go in — bang! It all goes sky high. Now that will make a real good story, won't it?

SCENE FOUR

(*Back on the site the housewives are gathered in a little group away from the sitting workmen*)

Mrs. Price. Look at them — the great lubbocks! Call themselves men!

Mrs. Wright. Great babies. Got to do what the council tells them. Sitting there waiting for their toy bulldozer so they can play at knocking down houses.

12

Mrs. Spencer. It isn't going to turn up. It's been pinched.

Mrs. Price. Grown men like you! Going to pull the house in on top of old Miss Ray are you?

Mrs. Marks. Ought to be ashamed of yourselves. What will your wives think when they see you on television tonight, destroying good homes?

Mrs. Spencer. Why don't you answer back?

(She picks up a clod of earth to throw. In a moment so do the others. The workmen scramble for cover)

Mrs. Spencer. You want to play at babies do you? Let's play then.

Foreman. Don't let 'em pick a fight! They'll stop after a bit.

Ginger. Go on. Let's chuck something back. A few bricks, eh?

Sammy. Stow it Ginger — that's just what they want! Look Boss, I don't reckon it would do any harm if we talked to them.

Foreman. You heard what Alliss said. It'll be on your head — I want no part of it. They'll not get me arguing. Ouch! That had a stone in.

Sammy. All right. It's my responsibility. Hey — stop a minute.

(He stands up and walks towards the angry women)

Sammy. Stop chucking things for a minute and listen will you?

Mrs. Marks. We'll listen. It's you lot that haven't been listening.

Mrs. Spencer. Had enough, have you?

Sammy. I want to talk with you.

Mrs. Marks. All right then — talk.

13

Sammy. Me and my mates — we reckon you've got the wrong people. We don't make the decisions. It's not fair to put any blame on us is it now?

Mrs. Price. That's no good. If you refused to do the work, it wouldn't matter what decision the council made. It's like wartime. Governments can only make war because they've got pilots willing to drop the bombs.

Mrs. Wright. You can't shuffle out of it. If we hadn't stopped you Miss Ray's house would have been a heap of dust by now — and it's you that would have done it. Nobody else.

Sammy. You can't think about everything. Every time we lift a shovel full of cement we can't be thinking 'are we doing the right thing?'. There isn't time.

Mrs. Marks. You've got time now. This morning you can think.

Sammy. Okay, so I'm thinking. I'm a navvy I am. I've worked on building sites for fourteen years. I like it. I get about. I've got some good mates. It's open-air, and there's a lot of laughs. It's well paid.

Ginger. Right. So shut up and get on with it.

Sammy. No, Ginger, it isn't so easy. I do wonder sometimes whether we're always doing the right things. Knocking down the old buildings, building great concrete motorways across the farmland. All for what?

Ginger. Progress, you great burk! Roads, flats, bridges! You want to live in a cave and have a club over your shoulder you do.

Sammy. No I don't. Things have got to change. But every time you knock something down to build something new — that's not progress *every* time. Remember when we worked on Chandler's Row, More? Worked on it together. Shifted all the families and knocked down two rows of little houses. Built a block of flats. That was eight years ago. Well, just before Easter I went back

14

there to knock part of the flats down to build a new flyover.

More. More cars. It's inevitable Sammy.

Sammy. Perhaps. I don't know. Point is — there'd have been room for the flyover if they'd just left the houses there in the first place. They ought to think ahead more — that's all I'm saying.

Ginger. Going over to the women are you Sammy?

Sammy. I think we should talk about it. Is it all right if we talk it over Blackbird?

Blackbird. The Union is always in favour of talks.

Foreman. Remember what Alliss said.

More. We're doing nothing daft. Just talking things over.

Sammy. Makes sense. Before I tear the roof down on any of those houses I want to be sure I'm in the right, that's all.

SCENE FIVE

(**Inspector Hargreaves** *looks across his desk at the smartly-dressed Woman before him. His expression is as cold as his filing cabinet*)

Hargreaves. Let me be crystal clear. You represent an organisation called the Carrigan Street Society. Your aim is to force an enquiry into the building of the last stage of the inner ring motorway by impeding the work of council employees.

Woman. If that means we want to stop them, yes. We do.

Hargreaves. And you have come to tell me of your illegal actions in order that *I* can take action?

15

Woman. I've come to tell you not to take any notice of the rumours you might hear. We aren't doing anything illegal.

Hargreaves. I take it that your society has not in fact planted a bomb in each house in Carrigan Street?

Woman. Of course not. We want to go on living in those houses.

Hargreaves. And the first house to be demolished does not contain a Miss Ray, as the Town Clerk seemed to think?

Woman. Oh yes, that's true. Miss Ray has lived there for thirty years.

Hargreaves. Has she been back in the house?

Woman. You'll have to ask her Inspector. How should I know that?

Hargreaves. Will you please do one thing for me? Will you please sit down? This is obviously going to be a difficult interview and I don't like you smirking down at me like that.

Woman. I'm sorry if I trouble you.

Hargreaves. And the bulldozer. You hi-jacked the truck bearing the council bulldozer.

Woman. Nothing of the kind. The man who drives the truck called in to the Bridgate Cafe this morning about a quarter past eight — he often does that when there's a lot of traffic — and somebody told him to drive his truck to a different destination. The silly man didn't even check up whether the new instructions were genuine.

Hargreaves. And I suppose you don't know who did that?

Woman. No idea, Inspector.

Hargreaves. And where is the bulldozer going?

Woman. Land's End.

Hargreaves. Land's End? Look, this really has gone past a joke. Your society has invited press and television down to Carrigan Street, hoping that you'll get as much publicity as possible for your silly schemes. Then people will say they admire your courage. We shall look fools. And you'll hold up the motorway for a month. You really are very selfish.

Woman. We had no other choice Inspector.

Hargreaves. Of course you had. You could have written, or 'phoned, or seen your Member of Parliament. There are a hundred ways of making a protest. This isn't a police state.

Woman. There are a hundred ways of protesting, but there's only one way of making sure anybody takes any notice. That's by taking action, by doing something about it instead of just meekly going off to live in a block of flats five miles away.

Hargreaves. Are the council workmen actually on the site at this moment?

Woman. Oh yes, and so are the women from the street. And the press and television boys should be arriving about now.

Hargreaves. I rather think I ought to go down to Carrigan Street. And I think you should come with me. From all you tell me I think it quite likely there will be a riot!

SCENE SIX

(The street is filling up. Several arguments break out, and there is much cheering and booing. As the argument develops the television crew and the press reporters appear and start filming and taking notes)

Foreman. Don't talk such drivel! You got to change human nature first. A man wants his own car, wants the freedom to go where he chooses . . .

17

Mrs. Price. What about the freedom to live where he chooses?

Foreman. We're not talking about that.

Ginger. We were talking about cars, you stupid old ratbag.

Mrs. Marks. What's free about a hundred men sitting in a hundred cars all jammed up every morning round the war memorial? What's free about being in a traffic jam, with the fumes rusting your lungs away and your blood pressure going up every minute . . .

Foreman. The new roads get rid of traffic jams.

Mrs. Wright. Don't be so simple! More people bring their cars out. Makes bigger traffic jams, that's all. Ban cars and make people ride in buses, I say. You can get fifty people in a bus.

More. It's not as if you were being thrown out on the street. Council's built them flats for you.

Mrs. Marks. You're joking. Do you know what it's like? You leave your own house and go five miles away where you don't know anybody, and the kids don't know anybody and your old man's got to take a fifteen pence bus ride to work. Kids have to start a different school. You have to start with a different milkman and butcher, and a different doctor and everything. Well you get a flat – maybe it's on the fourth floor. One of them where you've got to walk two miles if you've forgotten to bring the milk in, and where you get dizzy looking out of the lav window. First your furniture don't fit. You got to try and save for new curtains, and new carpets. You got to buy a new electric cooker because the street was all gas and this is all electricity . . .

Mrs. Francis. Do you know what finally did for me when I saw one of those flats? On the wall there's a knob you twist to turn the heating up and down. And by the side of it there's a notice, and do you know what it says? 'Tenants are particularly requested to close all windows when the red light is on'. It didn't say please. It didn't even tell you *why* you had to do it. It just told you to close your own windows.

Mrs. Maloney. It is up to you. We're all in it together. The men who write the letters and the councillors and the workmen and the town clerk and everybody. We can stop things if we want. We can change things.

Sammy. We're thinking missus. You've given us plenty to think about.

Foreman. Well, I've done my thinking. Alliss is coming back in a minute, I reckon. Are you lot going to stay with me and do the job you're paid to do — or are you going to join that gaggle of cackling women?

(Sharp blast on the whistle)

More. Come on Blackbird, spit it out.

Blackbird. You can't stop a worker from following his own conscience.

Foreman. Don't talk such rubbish. You've got a conscience after you knock off at five o'clock and not before. Look on your pay slip Blackbird, at what it says. 'Worker' that's what it says. Or perhaps on yours it says 'Thinker'? Perhaps they pay you for your brains, is that it?

Blackbird. That's what Hitler taught. That's wrong. A working man has got the right to think. Like a scientist. Or a teacher. You've not always got to follow the book.

Sammy. What's come over you Blackbird? Is it a full moon or something? I thought you lived by the book, worked to rules all the time. We all reckoned you used to have the Union Handbook for breakfast instead of Shredded Wheat.

Blackbird. There comes a time when you've got to think for yourself. You can't trust authority, I've always said that.

Foreman. Are you going over to their side then Blackbird?

Blackbird. Yes, I think I am.

19

Ginger. You rat! You stinking rat! Leave your own mates would you?

(Sensing conflict, the television crew spring into action, unnoticed . . .)

Blackbird. Get out of my way Ginger. That's a reasonable request.

Ginger. I'll smash your face in, you two faced little squirt . . .

Blackbird. I've got a right. I can think for myself. Change my mind.

Ginger. You haven't got any rights. Only thing you're fit for is a lot of stupid women.

More. Leave him alone Ginger.

Blackbird. I'll get you for assault. I've got witnesses. I'll get it in black and white.

Ginger. You ought to have a handbag and a powder puff! Never mind black and white, you'll be black and blue when I've done with you . . .

Blackbird. Don't touch me. I'm warning you.

Ginger. You great soft nellie!

(He throws himself at **Blackbird** *who fights back furiously)*

Foreman. Stop it you two. Don't be so thick! Its just what they want you to do.

Sammy. Throw a bucket of cold water over them! Hold their arms!

(The other workmen drag them apart, their fists still flailing)

Ginger. I'll tie him up in knots, the great prat!

Blackbird. It'll be a court case. You've had it now. You'll get three months!

Sammy. Calm down, both of you. Stow it.

Blackbird. I got witnesses.

Foreman. Too right you got witnesses. Look over there – look who was watching all the time you two madmen was scrapping.

(The television cameras are whirring; the pressmen write eagerly)

Foreman. You could not have done anything more stupid if you'd tried. All that performance on film – every minute of it.

Sammy. You shouldn't have let him rile you Blackbird. You want to laugh at people. Don't take it so serious.

Foreman. That's really done it that has. That's really torn it. Whatever happens now we're going to look a lot of fools. Look at them women smiling. I don't blame 'em. Whatever happens, we're going to get it in the neck!

SCENE SEVEN

*(The **Editor** has shown out the representatives of the Carrigan Street Society and is now taking a few moments off to do the crossword. His Secretary is sitting at a table at the further end of the large room)*

Editor. P.E.R.S.U.A.D.E. I thought that was it. I must say that I am taking longer and longer each day to do the crossword in my own paper. Do you think they're getting harder Carol, or is it because I am getting too old?

Carol. I think they're getting harder sir.

Editor. How very tactful of you. Now this is eight letters and the second letter is U. 'A Keeper's newspaper. Might be on sentry go'. What on earth is that do you think?

21

Carol. Something to do with castles? A dungeon?

Editor. Alas no, it doesn't fit. I'll put it aside and perhaps it will come to me when I'm thinking of something else. What have we during the next hour?

Carol. Well Mr. Alliss has been waiting to see you for forty minutes.

Editor. So he has. Do you know Mr. Alliss, Carol? He's a young man, and very keen to get on in the world. He works in the Architect's Department, and I rather fancy he's a member of my club.

Carol. Do you know what he wants to see you about?

Editor. Oh yes, he wants to see me about the new inner ring road. Those people that just left have got one or two little surprises in store for the council. Our Mr. Alliss, unless I am very much mistaken, wants to make sure we won't print anything to help them. He will give me the official council position.

Carol. Do you want me to stay?

Editor. Call him up now, and leave us alone for five minutes or so.

(She speaks into the intercom)

Carol. Could Mr. Alliss come up please? The Editor will see him for five minutes.

Editor. Who is down at the Carrigan Street site at the moment?

Carol. Mike Carraway and two staff photographers. And I think the Sports Editor went a few minutes ago.

Editor. Did he? Well, I gather that the television people are there as well. They'll be charging admission soon.

(An urgent knock on the door)

Editor. Ah, Mr. Alliss I fancy. Oh Carol, while you're out do get Charlie

Patrick to do an artist's impression of what it will look like when
the motorway is finished. We might be able to use it later. And let
Mr. Alliss in, will you?

(She goes; **Alliss** *bursts in the room)*

Editor. Ah, John dear boy, how nice to see you! I haven't had a
moment free before. How good of you to wait.

Alliss. That girl you've got in reception is a menace. For half an hour
she has been telling me, kick for kick, every detail of the game last
night.

Editor. She does talk a lot. I'm so sorry you've been bored.

Alliss. Its just that I'm in a tearing hurry. I've come about this rumpus
over Carrigan Street. You've just been seeing some of their people,
I gather. Well, I do want to put the other side of the picture to
you. Everyone at the Council was most anxious I should make
certain that you had the facts.

Editor. Your view of the facts. Yes, I understand. Well, I am listening
carefully. What are the facts?

Alliss. That we wish to do something urgent to relieve the traffic
problem in the centre. We believe that it is in everybody's interest
to do so.

Editor. In the interests of car users certainly. Go on.

Alliss. And once started on the inner ring road scheme, we feel that it is
in everybody's interest that it is completed as soon as possible.

Editor. In time for the May Elections, yes. And now these dreadful
people are playing games with your project and you've been held
up.

Alliss. This isn't just playing games. Its wasting time, money and
manpower. We've got men sitting down there doing nothing . . .

Editor. Just like ourselves, Mr. Alliss . . .

Alliss. They are standing in the way of progress. That motorway schem is forward-looking.

Editor. Now there I am not altogether sure I agree with you. Tell me John, have you ever been out to my house in Cherry Wood?

Alliss. No. I never have.

Editor. A pity. You must come out some time. Do you play bridge? No? Well, I suppose it is a game for elderly men like myself. The point however about Cherry Wood is that fifteen years ago they built the municipal airport on the other side of the copse – said i was essential. On that occasion I was one of the protestors – but didn't do any good.

Alliss. What has that to do with Carrigan Street?

Editor. I brought up my children in the din of aircraft – all hours of the day and night. My poor wife has had to take sleeping pills for ten years and we've never been able to open a window without being deafened by the planes. But you know, it only seemed to d really good business for a year or two. And now they're closing it down.

Alliss. Yes I know. Not a paying concern.

Editor. Simply the wrong sort of place. Now it's all jumbo jets, and va airports miles from anywhere like Foulness. Got to have big airports – not tiny little places scattered all over the countryside And the moral is – they didn't think ahead far enough.

Alliss. And you think that the council hasn't thought far enough into the future?

Editor. That may be so – I'm not sure. It takes hundreds of years to build a large place like ours – its very easy to destroy a town quickly though. It may be – it *may* be that you're not thinking the thing through. In fifty years' time they'll probably be cursing you.

24

Alliss. Is that what the people from the society said?

Editor. Not exactly.

Alliss. All I hope is that you will print both sides to the question, that's all.

Editor. Of course. The *Post* is always fair. We have two aims. One is to be first with the news, and beat the *Evening Star,* and the other is always to be fair.

Alliss. I think I'll get back to the site, then.

Editor. I think I will come with you. I've got a feeling that things are getting near to a crisis.

Alliss. I've got one bit of news for you. Adamson, the Town Clerk, is going down there to tell them to ignore the women and to get on with destroying the houses.

Editor. And I have a little news for you. Apparently the man who was transporting the bulldozer is on his way to the site. He rang up Head Office for further directions and found it had all been a hoax. So there — the Town Clerk, the bulldozer and the Carrigan Street Society. Quite an explosive situation!

(On the intercom)

Editor. Carol, I'm going out. Down to Carrigan Street. Yes, do hold the front page . . .

SCENE EIGHT

(The street is crowded, and crackles with tension. The groups sit and stand eyeing each other warily
Adamson *arrives puffed, his secretary with him. Shortly afterwards from a different direction come* **Hargreaves** *and the*

25

Woman. *Finally the* **Editor** *arrives with* **Alliss)**

Foreman. On your feet lads — it's the Town Clerk.

Adamson. Just a minute — I'm puffed. Been running. I shall have to take one of my pills.

(As **Adamson** *tries to take charge of the situation, there is growing anger in the crowd. Some close in on him)*

Adamson. There — that's better. Now Foreman, what on earth is going on here? Why hasn't the work begun?

Foreman. Well we had some trouble with the bulldozer.

Adamson. But that's arrived now, I hope. It has? We can go into who was responsible for such a childish trick later. There may have to be a court case. I've got two bailiffs and a woman police constable coming down.

Foreman. Good. Time we had some order.

Adamson. Its time we got those old houses down. According to the work schedule it should only take a day to pull down the houses and two days for clearance. The council does not pay wages for men to sit on their backsides and talk over their work with the local women.

(Sharp blast on the whistle)

Adamson. Heavens! What on earth is that dreadful row?

Blackbird. I think you should know Mr. Adamson that one or two of the council employees are by no means satisfied. The Union demands the right to let the men talk it over, this job.

Ginger. You mean you demand it. I don't. Lots of the blokes don't care what the job is; do you?

Adamson. Do I understand then that some employees are refusing to undertake this work. Are you refusing to do it?

Blackbird. I am. I'm willing to do another job but not this – not until there's been an enquiry.

Adamson. You are a very stupid man. You realise that you will probably be sacked.

Blackbird. You can't sack me. It's a matter of conscience.

Adamson. And who is joining you in this?

Sammy. I am, Mr. Adamson.

Adamson. Anyone else?

Sammy. Ginger? More? Isn't there anybody else with any courage?

Adamson. They have too much sense. Right then, now we'll get to work.

(A policewoman enters, with two burly-looking bailiffs)

Adamson. There has been too much talk and not enough action. Now you three. I want that door broken in and I should like you Policewoman Smith, to go inside and escort Miss Ray from the premises – if she's in there.

Mrs. Maloney. Shame on you. All of you!

Mrs. Francis. We want a public enquiry. Hands off Carrigan Street!

(The bailiffs prepare as Hargreaves *arrives)*

Adamson. I want no undue violence. But please remember all of you that what we are entering is council property. If you are sensible nobody will get hurt.

Hargreaves. What's happening here Town Clerk?

Adamson. They are entering the house sir, to make sure it is unoccupied.

Woman. Can they do this Inspector?

Hargreaves. Of course they can. It is council property. They can do exactly what they like with it.

(The crowd begins chanting. Others catcall)

Crowd. Hands — off — Carrigan-Street! Hands — off — Carrigan-Street!

Woman. Just think of what Miss Ray must be feeling now.

Hargreaves. Think of the ratepayers' money that's being wasted by this pantomime.

Woman. Have you no sympathy for them at all?

Hargreaves. None at all.

Adamson. Right men — I'll give her just one last chance.

(He walks up to the door)

Adamson. Is anyone in there? Do you hear me? I want you to come out. If you do not I shall ask these men to break in the door by force. It will be much easier for you if you come out now.

Sammy. No answer. You've got to admire her spirit.

Hargreaves. I don't believe anyone is in there.

Editor. I agree with you Inspector. At least I think I do.

Alliss. Hoping for a good story are you?

Editor. I am certainly not hoping for Miss Ray's death, if that is what you mean. No, I'm hoping the Society doesn't give way.

Adamson. All right men, break in.

(They put their shoulders down. After three tries the barred door splinters open and they go cautiously in; W. P. C. Smith follows them)

Mrs. Wright. I hope you television lads are getting all this down.

Mrs. Marks. And the people from the papers. You heard what he said. Our homes destroyed in one day.

Editor. Have no fear dear lady. The *Post* is here.

Adamson. Now come on all of you — the fun's over. You've made a bit of a fuss. You've got your names in the papers. You can all go home now.

(The three come out of the house)

Adamson. Well, what did you find?

W. P. C. Smith. There's no-one there. We searched all through the house but we couldn't find anyone.

Hargreaves. Any signs of recent occupation Smith?

W. P. C. Smith. Oh yes sir. Somebody has certainly been in there recently. They've had a lantern. With the windows boarded up it's a bit dark, but I think furniture's been moved recently. Some old tables and chairs in there.

Editor. And you saw signs that meals had been eaten?

W. P. C. Smith. No sign of that, no.

Adamson. Right, well if there's no one in there we can get on with it. At least we'll have the first outhouse and wall down. Mr. Alliss.

Alliss. Yes, Mr. Adamson.

Adamson. I think that as soon as we get to work all this will blow over. I want you to help me get things started. Take three men off and start moving up the bulldozer. We'll take the first wall down with picks and shovels. Foreman! Over here!

Foreman. Yes sir.

Adamson. Gather the men together here and make a start on the outer wall. Quick as you can.

Foreman. Right men, get the picks. You start up there. You others down here. Push them butresses up so it falls inwards.

Adamson. And the rest of you can go now. It is all over. There is nobody in the house and the men will just be working for the rest of the day.

Foreman. Right men, put your backs into it.

(It is all action; the men hacking at the wall and moving the wooden butresses so it caves inwards
In the crowd arguments break out; the **Editor** *checks camera angles with his staff*
The **Television reporter** *interviews* **Hargreaves**

Interviewer. Would it be fair, in your opinion, to describe the incidents today as a storm in a teacup.

Hargreaves. Certainly. The Society had worked out a few tricks to try to stop the work going ahead, but I believe everything is now going according to plan.

Interviewer. You're not expecting any further trouble then?

Hargreaves. I sincerely hope not.

Interviewer. Thank you Inspector. Well, I think that the first wall of the end house is about to cave in. Let's just watch.

(He turns. With a rumble, then a screaming explosion, the wall

collapses inwards in a mushroom cloud of choking dust. There is a
silence, and for the first time the crowd stands still)

Alliss. That's it then — the first step.

Woman. Are you pleased with yourself then?

Foreman. I shall be when I get the whole street down Miss. When I do a
job I do it properly.

(The interviewer speaks in hushed tones)

Interviewer. And so that looks like the end of the affair. I get the
impression that there will be no enquiry. The efforts of the
Carrigan Street Society seem to have failed.

Woman. Aren't you forgetting about the cellars?

Adamson. Cellars? I didn't know there were cellars. Alliss — are there
cellars in these houses?

Alliss. Oh yes sir. Its all on the plans. All the houses in Carrigan Street
have cellars.

Adamson. Did you know this Foreman?

Foreman. I was following your orders in getting that wall down. I
didn't have time to look at the plans.

Hargreaves. Smith! When you went into the house did you look in the
cellars?

W. P. C. Smith. I didn't see any cellars sir.

Hargreaves. Did the bailiffs?

Bailiffs. No.

Adamson. Well how on earth did you miss them out?

Woman. I think I can help, Town Clerk. Miss Ray used to sometimes pull a chest of drawers down the hall in front of the cellar door. In the poor light you could easily miss it.

Mrs. Francis. That's right. I've gone in there sometimes and she's been in the cellar and I've hardly been able to see the door. Could hardly see to open it.

Alliss. She went down the cellar often?

Woman. Oh yes, often.

Adamson. But if nobody looked down there . . .

(He turns towards the crumpled wall)

Sammy. You've probably pulled the wall in on top of her! That's what you were going to say . . .

Adamson. Stop those cameras! This is serious.

Sammy. Don't just stand there you fool — lets clear it — and quick!

Blackbird. You've killed her! Now you've done it. You've killed her!

Adamson. I thought they were bluffing. After all, the bulldozer was just a hoax, and the bomb story. I thought this was too . . . Oh Stanley, where are my pills.

Sammy. Come on the rest of you — shift this rubbish!

Hargreaves. Get the Ambulance. Stand back if you're not helping.

(Feverishly the crowd begins to pull at the pile of rubbish. Every minute the Foreman puts up a hand and the crowd listens for a sound)

Mrs. Maloney. Murder! That's what it is — cold-blooded murder.

Interviewer. The Carrigan Street affair has this afternoon taken a new and ugly turn. Immediately after the demolition began there were fears that Miss Ray, one of the residents of the street, had in fact been accidentally buried in her own home. Behind me the workmen and spectators are scrambling to clear away the mountain of bricks and mortar that was once Miss Ray's home. Meanwhile, I have one of the residents by my side. You are a member of the Carrigan Street Society I believe.

Woman. Yes, I am.

Interviewer. And what is your reaction to the council's behaviour today?

Woman. I think they're frightened. Frightened to let people really have a say in their own futures.

Interviewer. Just a minute. Standing back to watch the rescue attempts I have the town clerk by my side. Mr. Adamson, how are the rescue attempts going?

Adamson. As well as can be expected.

Interviewer. Am I right in thinking that the protests of the Carrigan Street Society are all because you will not allow an enquiry.

Adamson. The council refused in the first place. It wasn't my decision.

Interviewer. But now, I imagine, there will have to be an enquiry. In view of all that has happened here today, and in view of all the publicity there will be?

Adamson. Yes, there will be one. I think the council will do that.

Interviewer. And so, in a way, the Society will have got its wish. It is however a tragedy that a human life may have been in danger before that happened. Miss Ray could in fact have been the martyr of Carrigan Street.

Woman. I don't think so.

Interviewer. I didn't quite catch that.

Woman. What you and Mr. Adamson don't know you see is that Miss Ray is perfectly safe.

Adamson. Why on earth didn't you tell us before?

Woman. I had to wait until you said that there would be an enquiry. And you can't get out of it now — it's on the television film.

Adamson. But — how do you know this? Where is she?

Woman. She's here, that's how I know. I am Margaret Ray. I have lived in Carrigan Street since I was born. Even after the death of my parents I went on living there. I liked the area Mr. Adamson.

Adamson. Another trick!

(He shouts to the crowd)

Adamson. Stop that! Miss Ray's all right — she's here! They've been fooling us again.

Ginger. I'd like to get at her. Making a fool of me!

Foreman. That's a relief, that is . . .

Woman. Ladies and Gentleman, you will be pleased to know that the Town Clerk has said that there will now be an enquiry. We may lose — they may decide to build the motorway after all — but we shall have won our point. I know that we've had to play a set of rather childish tricks, but the point about them was that they *could* have been more serious than they were. What we made you realise what that ordinary people *do* have power. They can change things. They can make their voices heard.

Adamson. It was a stupid way to go about it.

Woman. But it worked, didn't it? And perhaps it has taught us all that we have go to try a bit harder when we change things to make sure

34

we're making them better — not just doing what seems most convenient. And the officials perhaps ought to see that they should trust people more. We've got to work things out together! The people in the council offices aren't our guardians, they're our servants!

(She steps down to cheers, and some boos. The crowd splits up. We hear several fragments of conversation)

Adamson. We'll hold it up for a fortnight. Put the men on other work.

Foreman. What about Blackbird, Mr. Adamson? And Sammy?

Adamson. They're sacked. Now get the men off the site.

Foreman. All right lads, get your gear together. We're moving off.

Stanley. Shall I write and tell the Mayor, Mr. Adamson?

Adamson. Yes. Let's get back to the office. I need another pill.

(The men gather their things and move away)

Mrs. Marks. We won then; a triumph for democracy.

Hargreaves. Believe that if you like madam. Personally I suspect that you just wanted to make nuisances of yourselves. You know you'll lose in the long run.

(The women leave, chattering together . . .)

Editor. Well Miss Ray I congratulate you. You are a born showman. Poor Mr. Alliss looks very sorry for himself.

Woman. Thank you. I hope the *Post* will give us a fair report.

Editor. It certainly will. But do you mind me asking one thing? You allowed them to destroy part of your own house. What happens if you win your appeal and are allowed to return here?

Woman. I'm leaving. I've a new job in London. As a matter of fact I'm hoping to be a reporter myself.

Editor. Are you indeed? Well, you will have one good story won't you?

Woman. I hope you don't believe I did it for that reason.

Editor. I never really know who to trust, I'm afraid. That is because I've been a reporter myself for so long. Speaking for myself I shall just go back to my office and complete my crossword. Goodbye Miss Ray. I hope you will find other good causes.

(They shake hands and part; only **Blackbird** *and* **Sammy** *are left)*

Blackbird. I shall fight it. It's illegal to sack me.

Sammy. Don't worry so much Blackbird. Take to the road. Plenty of labouring to be done.

*(***Nevis** *is hobbling towards them)*

Sammy. Well look who the cat's dragged in. I didn't know it was that late.

Nevis. It isn't. I heard about it all on the one o'clock news. You can't say I didn't warn you.

*(***Blackbird** *is waiting;* **Sammy** *goes to get his coat)*

Sammy. No. You warned me all right.

Nevis. Sounded as if there was going to be a riot.

Sammy. Well there wasn't.

Nevis. What happened to all them protestors?

Sammy. Oh, they turned the hoses on 'em, loaded 'em in police vans and threw 'em into the dungeons.

Nevis. Don't talk so daft! What's the matter with you — can't you ever be serious?

Sammy. Sometimes Ben, sometimes . . .

(He walks slowly off)

selected titles
dramascripts

Topical plays

Adam's Ark
Harold Hodgson
0-333-18244-8

Carrigan Street
John Pick
0-333-13874-0

Frankly Frankie
Rony Robinson
0-333-35895-3

Hijack
Charles Wells
0-333-13873-2

Panel Games
Eileen Brandon
(and) **The Headmistress
and the Minister**
O. A. Jones
0-333-30104-8

The Terrible Fate of Humpty Dumpty
David Calcutt
0-333-39589-1

Unman, Wittering and Zigo
Giles Cooper
0-333-12925-3

Adaptations of Classics

A Christmas Carol
Charles Dickens
0-333-14401-5

Oliver Twist
Charles Dickens
0-333-06781-9

Pip and the Convict
Charles Dickens
0-333-12501-0

A Tale of Two Cities
Charles Dickens
0-333-38384-2

Far from the Madding Crowd
Thomas Hardy
0-333-37690-0

The Mayor of Casterbridge
Thomas Hardy
0-333-30833-6

Tom Sawyer
Mark Twain
0-333-19556-6

Huckleberry Finn
Mark Twain
0-333-37691-9

Treasure Island
Robert Louis Stevenson
0-333-33443-4

The Wind in the Willows
Kenneth Grahame
0-333-39738-X

Plays from other sources

The Machine-Gunners
Robert Westall
0-333-39645-6

The Brick
(and)
After the Party
David Williams
0-333-36399-X

Sir Gawain and the Green K
Adapted by David Self
0-333-26609-9

The Doctor and the Devils
Dylan Thomas
0-333-10411-0

The Government Inspector
Nicolai Gogol
0-333-28490-9

The Iliad of Homer
Kenneth Cavander
0-333-24484-2

The Odyssey of Homer
Kenneth Cavander
0-333-24485-0